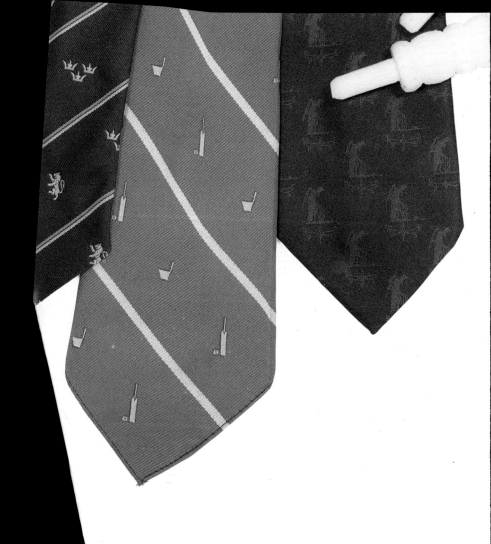

Published by Ebury Press
National Magazine House
72 Broadwick Street
London W1V 2BP

First impression 1984
A PHOEBE PHILLIPS EDITIONS BOOK
Copyright © Phoebe Phillips Editions 1984

ISBN 0 85223 415 5

Filmset by Battley Brothers

Printed and bound in Italy by Sagdos

Vic Lewis

CRICKET
TIES

An Interna'
Cri

Contents

Introduction

From the beginning of history some kind of signal or distinguishing mark, be it a shield, a hair-style or a special robe, has identified groups who have interests in common – members of a regiment, a religious sect, even followers of a particular fashion. Cricket ties are simply a modern version of this, and a very colourful signal they make, too.

I started collecting ties in 1952, when I first joined Derbyshire C.C. and was proud to wear the team's colours. Since I was a band-leader, and many players were interested in what I was doing, it was relatively easy to obtain other ties associated with cricket. Now, with the help of many friends, I have well over 3,000 in my collection. I started my own cricket team partly as a result of this generosity, so that when someone gave me a tie I could give them one in return.

The first cricket club tie, issued in 1863, was for the Eton Ramblers (page 39). Originally, most cricket ties were variations on a theme: stripes in different colours, all running diagonally down the tie.

Crests and motifs were mass-produced for the first time in the 1920s, and nowadays many ties feature the woven motifs that add so much symbolic interest: variations of city or borough crests, combinations of cricketing paraphernalia such as crossed bats with stumps, and so on.

Background colours are open to choice and have no restrictions whatsoever. For example, the colours of my Vic Lewis C.C. tie are based on the following criteria: green for the colour of the cricket ground; blue for the jazz blues played by my band; and mauve because it is my favourite colour.

Cricket history has many shadowy corners, and I would like to thank my editors and my friends for their help in amassing information (both oral and written) for the captions. I would also like to thank Messrs. T. M. Lewin of Jermyn Street, London, Dave Mackay Ties, and indeed cricket-lovers every- where who support their local clubs.

Any selection I could make from such a store of riches would be open to accusations of favouritism; there is no denying that this is a personal choice, where the interest of the motif, the design and the colour as well as international appeal have all been considerations.

Those whose tie is not included will be patient, I hope, and a second volume may join this first modest celebration of one of the traditional symbols of English sporting life.

Above: Lord's cricket ground is named after
Thomas Lord (right), who owned the M.C.C.'s
original ground and hired it to the club. The
M.C.C. bought the turf, which was moved twice
before being settled at St John's Wood in London.

M.C.C. City. This tie
was created because
City businessmen
required a tie that
would not clash with
their sober apparel.

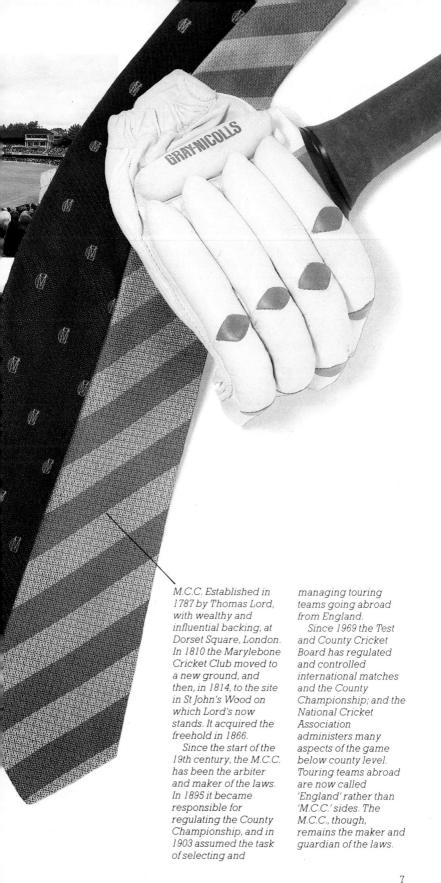

M.C.C. Established in 1787 by Thomas Lord, with wealthy and influential backing, at Dorset Square, London. In 1810 the Marylebone Cricket Club moved to a new ground, and then, in 1814, to the site in St John's Wood on which Lord's now stands. It acquired the freehold in 1866.

Since the start of the 19th century, the M.C.C. has been the arbiter and maker of the laws. In 1895 it became responsible for regulating the County Championship, and in 1903 assumed the task of selecting and managing touring teams going abroad from England.

Since 1969 the Test and County Cricket Board has regulated and controlled international matches and the County Championship; and the National Cricket Association administers many aspects of the game below county level. Touring teams abroad are now called 'England' rather than 'M.C.C.' sides. The M.C.C., though, remains the maker and guardian of the laws.

M.C.C. 'B' CLUB TOURING. Awarded to members of teams touring overseas on other than official first-class tours.

M.C.C. YOUNG CRICKETERS. The 1983 version of the 'Nippers' tie for young players, usually promising cricketers on probation. They generally help with ground duties at Lord's.

*THE NATIONAL
CRICKET
ASSOCIATION.
Responsible, since
1969, for regulating
most aspects of the
game in England
below County and
Minor County level. It
was set up in 1965 as
the M.C.C. Cricket
Association.*

YOUNG ENGLAND.
Tie awarded to
cricketers under 19
who have been
capped to play in an
international match.
Players are selected
from the 35 counties
affiliated to the
National Association of
Young Cricketers.

ENGLAND (touring).
Tie given to cricketers
who play for England
overseas in Test
matches.

ENGLAND (at home).
Tie given to cricketers
chosen to play, at
home, in Test matches.

Like the England ties on the previous page, these are awarded to cricketers who have been chosen to play for their country in Test matches.

AUSTRALIA

PAKISTAN

INDIA
(Jubilee tie)

SRI LANKA

NEW ZEALAND

WEST INDIES

Below: The Melbourne cricket ground, the largest in the world, and the venue for the 1956 Olympic Games. The picture shows the 1975 3rd Test between Australia and the West Indies.

ADMINISTRATION

INTERNATIONAL CRICKET CONFERENCE; 1909, as the Imperial Cricket Conference. The title was changed in 1965 to reflect a more international membership than the original 3 of England, Australia and South Africa. Representatives of the current 7 members – Australia, England, India, New Zealand, Pakistan, Sri Lanka and the West Indies – meet every year at Lord's, as the governing body for cricket.

CLUB CRICKET CONFERENCE; 1915, by a sports journalist to band together London and southern counties teams. Now the official body of cricket clubs in this region.

I.C.C. ASSOCIATES:
1965, to accommodate
the growing number of
cricket-playing
countries, some of
whom were not
eligible for full I.C.C.
membership. The first
3 associates were Fiji,
the U.S.A. and Ceylon
(now Sri Lanka and
elevated to full I.C.C.
membership).

**MINOR COUNTIES
CRICKET
ASSOCIATION:** 1895, in
Birmingham for all
counties not in the first-
class list. Only 3
counties have moved
to first-class since then:
Worcestershire,
Northamptonshire and
Glamorgan.

HOLLAND (Players);
admitted as an I.C.C.
Associate Member in
1966. The Netherlands
Cricket Association
was formed in 1883.
Cricket is regularly
played against
Denmark. Some sides
play the M.C.C. at
Lord's. Holland took
part in the 1979 and
1982 I.C.C. Trophy
competitions.

PAPUA NEW GUINEA;
admitted 1973. Cricket
was introduced by
missionaries and
played mainly around
Port Moresby. The
Cricket Association
was formed in 1972
and Papua New
Guinea played in the
1979 and 1982 I.C.C.
Trophy competitions.

UNITED STATES; one
of 3 countries admitted
in 1965. Cricket has
been played for over
200 years, although the
first international
match, between
America and Canada,
did not take place until
1844, and the first
match against England
only in 1859. Played in
the 1979 and 1982 I.C.C.
Trophy competitions.

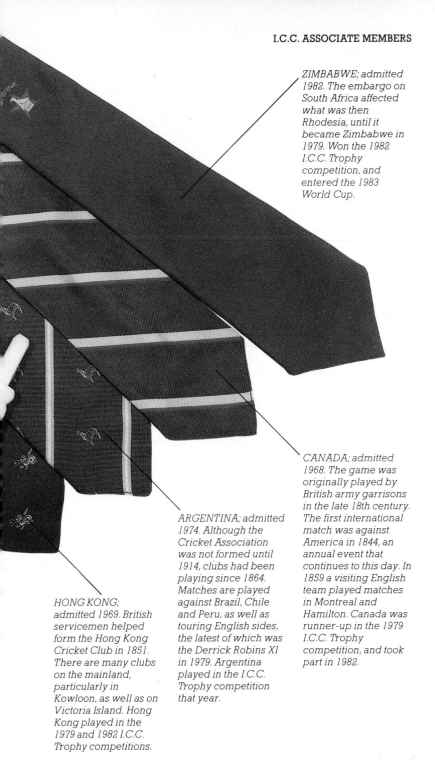

ZIMBABWE; admitted 1982. The embargo on South Africa affected what was then Rhodesia, until it became Zimbabwe in 1979. Won the 1982 I.C.C. Trophy competition, and entered the 1983 World Cup.

CANADA; admitted 1968. The game was originally played by British army garrisons in the late 18th century. The first international match was against America in 1844, an annual event that continues to this day. In 1859 a visiting English team played matches in Montreal and Hamilton. Canada was runner-up in the 1979 I.C.C. Trophy competition, and took part in 1982.

ARGENTINA; admitted 1974. Although the Cricket Association was not formed until 1914, clubs had been playing since 1864. Matches are played against Brazil, Chile and Peru, as well as touring English sides, the latest of which was the Derrick Robins XI in 1979. Argentina played in the I.C.C. Trophy competition that year.

HONG KONG; admitted 1969. British servicemen helped form the Hong Kong Cricket Club in 1851. There are many clubs on the mainland, particularly in Kowloon, as well as on Victoria Island. Hong Kong played in the 1979 and 1982 I.C.C. Trophy competitions.

BERMUDA; admitted as an I.C.C. Associate Member in 1966. Originally played by British army garrisons in the 1840s, the game soon became popular with Bermudans. Matches against American teams date from 1905. The island's major teams, Somerset and St George's, have played an annual Cup match since 1902. Took part in the 1979 and 1982 I.C.C. Trophy competitions.

FIJI; admitted 1965. Cricket was first played in the late 1880s by the British. A team toured New Zealand in 1895. Fiji was visited by a full English side in 1984. Played in 1979 and 1982 I.C.C. Trophy competitions.

SINGAPORE; admitted 1974. Has sent teams abroad, at first to Shanghai and Hong Kong, since the 1890s. Has received visits from touring sides en route to Australasia. The Singapore Cricket Association was formed in 1949. Played in the 1979 and 1982 I.C.C. Trophy competitions.

EAST AFRICAN CRICKET CONFERENCE; admitted 1966. Oversees matches between Uganda, Zambia, Tanzania, Malawi and Kenya (now a separate national side). It sent a team to England for the I.C.C. Trophy competitions in 1979 and 1982.

DENMARK; admitted 1966. Cricket was first played in the early 19th century. The Danish Cricket Association was formed in 1953. The first European International, against Holland, was in 1955, and Denmark took part in the 1979 I.C.C. Trophy competition.

BANGLADESH; admitted as an I.C.C. Associate Member in 1977. Cricket was not played officially until several years after Bangladesh gained independence from Pakistan in 1972. An M.C.C. side played there in 1976-77. Played in the 1979 and 1982 I.C.C. Trophy competitions.

KENYA; admitted 1981. Originally part of the East African Cricket Conference, Kenya formed its own side in the late 1970s. It was the first side to be visited by a minor counties representative team, and played in the 1982 I.C.C. Trophy competition.

ISRAEL; admitted 1974. The Israeli Cricket League was formed in 1966, mainly by immigrants from Britain, India and South Africa. Cricket is played in most major cities, and Israel took part in the 1979 and 1982 I.C.C. Trophy competitions.

GIBRALTAR; admitted 1969. The Royal Navy started cricket here in the 19th century. Australian and many English county sides have toured Gibraltar. Took part in the I.C.C. Trophy competition in 1982.

MALAYSIA; admitted 1967. Cricket was introduced by the British in the early 19th century, and the Malaysian Cricket Association was formed in 1948. Many international sides have played in Penang and Kuala Lumpur. Malaysia played in the 1979 and 1982 I.C.C. Trophy competitions.

SURREY; 1845, in Guildford. Has won the County Championship 19 times, including 7 consecutive wins between 1952 and 1958. Won the Benson and Hedges Cup in 1974 and the NatWest Trophy in 1982. Over the years, famous cricketers have included Tom Hayward and Jack Hobbs, Peter May and Ken Barrington.

MIDDLESEX; 1864. County champions 9 times, 4 of these victories between 1976 and 1982. Gillette Cup winners 1977 and 1980, and Benson and Hedges Cup winner in 1983. Denis Compton and Bill Edrich were household names in the late 1940s. In 1947 Compton scored 3,816 runs and Edrich 3,539.

COUNTY CRICKET CHAMPIONSHIP. 1873 is taken as the date from which the Championship assumed its modern form; this conforms with the lists published in the M.C.C. Diary. In 1895 the Championship was placed on a new footing and made the responsibility of the M.C.C. In this book a county is credited with achieving the title even when it shared first place.

KENT; 1870, in Canterbury. Has won the Championship 7 times, the Gillette Cup twice and the Benson and Hedges Cup 3 times. Frank Woolley and Colin Cowdrey are possibly the most celebrated of many fine batsmen. Wicket-keeper-batsmen, a Kentish speciality, include Les Ames and Alan Knott.

Left: The Oval, Kennington, England's oldest ground: England played Australia here in 1880. The photograph shows the first Test, England v. the West Indies, 1973.

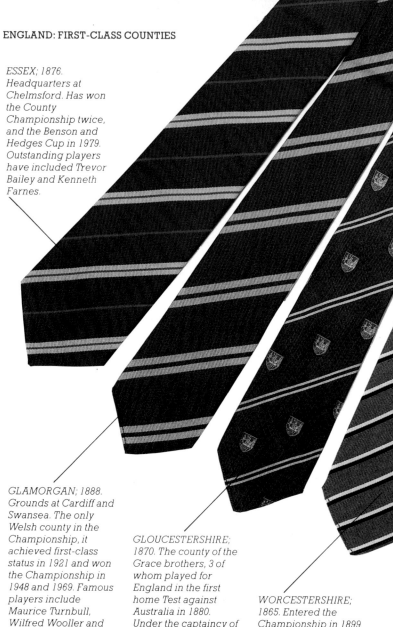

ESSEX; 1876. Headquarters at Chelmsford. Has won the County Championship twice, and the Benson and Hedges Cup in 1979. Outstanding players have included Trevor Bailey and Kenneth Farnes.

GLAMORGAN; 1888. Grounds at Cardiff and Swansea. The only Welsh county in the Championship, it achieved first-class status in 1921 and won the Championship in 1948 and 1969. Famous players include Maurice Turnbull, Wilfred Wooller and Tony Lewis (captain of England, 1972-73).

GLOUCESTERSHIRE; 1870. The county of the Grace brothers, 3 of whom played for England in the first home Test against Australia in 1880. Under the captaincy of W.G., Gloucestershire won the Championship 4 times between 1873 and 1877. In his career, W. G. Grace scored 54,896 runs and took 2,876 wickets. Later Walter Hammond became one of the world's greatest all-rounders. Gloucestershire won the Gillette Cup in 1973, the Benson and Hedges Cup in 1977.

WORCESTERSHIRE; 1865. Entered the Championship in 1899 and has won the title 3 times: in 1964, 1965 and 1974. Gillette Cup finalists in 1963 and 1966. The county's early success owed much to the Foster brothers. Between the wars, C. F. Walters and R. E. S. Wyatt both captained England. Two famous players from overseas are Basil d'Oliviera and Glenn Turner – the only post-war player to have made, in 1973, a thousand runs before the end of May.

SOMERSET; 1875. Main
ground at Taunton.
Admitted to the
Championship in 1891,
it is one of the 3
first-class counties still
to win it. Won the
Gillette Cup and
NatWest Trophy once
each, and the Benson
and Hedges Cup in
1981 and 1982. Great
players: Sammy
Woods, Jack White, Viv
Richards and Ian
Botham.

WARWICKSHIRE;
1882. Admitted to the
Championship in 1895,
it has won only 3 times
despite outstanding
players like Tom
Dollery, the first
professional captain of
a county (in 1948).
Notable current
players are Dennis
Amiss and Alvin
Kallicharan. Won the
Gillette Cup in 1966
and 1968. This is the
players' tie.

HAMPSHIRE; 1863, in
Southampton. Badge is
the Tudor rose and
crown. Cricket is
reputed to have started
at Hambledon. Entered
the Championship in
1895 and has won
twice, in 1961 and 1973.
Lord Tennyson,
grandson of the poet,
was a hard-hitting
batsman.

NORTHAMPTON-SHIRE; 1878. Admitted to first-class status in 1905. Never county champions, but won the Gillette Cup in 1976 and the Benson and Hedges Cup in 1980. Fine players include F. R. Brown (captain of England) in the 1950s, Colin Milburn in the 1960s and, today, Geoff Cook and Wayne Larkins.

NOTTINGHAMSHIRE; 1841. Won the County Championship 10 times between 1873 and 1900, but only 3 times since: in 1907, 1929 and 1981. Gary Sobers, arguably the greatest all-rounder in cricket's history, played regularly for the county until his retirement in 1974.

LEICESTERSHIRE; 1879. Admitted to the Championship in 1895, achieving the title for the first time in 1975. Won the Benson and Hedges Cup in 1972 and 1975. Maurice Hallam was probably the outstanding batsman in the 1950s and 1960s. Current star is David Gower, the England captain.

DERBYSHIRE; 1870. Lost first-class status in 1888, but regained it in 1894. Won the Championship in 1936. Winner of the NatWest Trophy in 1981. The Australian F. R. Spofforth captained the side in 1890, and South African Eddie Barlow 1976-78. Best-known current player is Bob Taylor, with more than 40 caps so far.

SUSSEX; 1839. Still to win the Championship. Won the Gillette Cup final in 1963 (the year of its inauguration), and again in 1964 and 1978. Its long list of distinguished players includes the great Ranjitsinhji, Maurice Tate between the wars, and John Snow in the 1960s and 1970s.

YORKSHIRE; 1863. Has won the Championship 30 times, last in 1968, the Gillette Cup in 1965 and 1969. Players must be born in the county. Outstanding cricketers: Lord Hawke, Herbert Sutcliffe, Sir Leonard Hutton (England's first professional captain) and, currently, Geoff Boycott.

LANCASHIRE; 1864. Won the Championship 5 times between 1879 and 1897 and 7 times between 1904 and 1950. Winners of the Gillette Cup 4 times and runners-up twice, 1970-76. Many fine players such as Walter Brearley in the 'Golden Age', George Duckworth in the late 1920s and the current captain, Clive Lloyd.

IRELAND. Cricket has
been played at
Phoenix Park since
1792. The Ireland
Cricket Union, formed
in 1923, has
representatives from
both Northern Ireland
and the Republic of
Ireland, and has had a
seat on the Cricket
Council since 1969.
Visiting teams have
included the West
Indies, who were
bowled out for 25 runs
in 1969. Distinguished
players include
A. J. O'Riordan and
J. C. Boucher. A few
cricketers have played
for English county
teams. Ireland
regularly takes part in
the NatWest Trophy.

WALES. Cricket has been played in the Principality since the 1780s, and Glamorgan is one of the 17 first-class counties. In 1979, when Gibraltar could not attend the I.C.C. Trophy competition, Wales was asked to enter a full team in its place. The good account it gave of itself was largely due to Bill Edwards, the manager. Among many fine Welsh cricketers Alan Watkins, Gilbert Parkhouse, Jim McConnon and Tony Lewis have all played at Test level.

SCOTLAND. Cricket has been played for over 200 years. The Scottish Cricket Union was formed in 1909 and Scotland now plays Ireland, the M.C.C. and touring sides in Britain. Famous cricketers who have gone on to play for England include Paul Gibb, Ian Peebles and Mike Denness, who captained England 1973-75. Scotland participates regularly in the Benson and Hedges Cup competition.

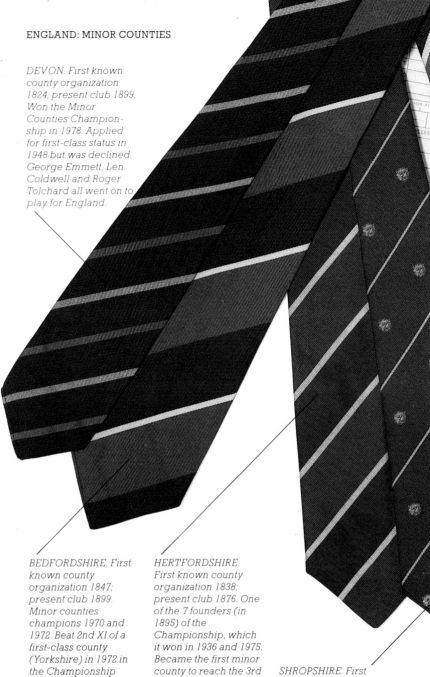

DEVON. First known county organization 1824; present club 1899. Won the Minor Counties Championship in 1978. Applied for first-class status in 1948 but was declined. George Emmett, Len Coldwell and Roger Tolchard all went on to play for England.

BEDFORDSHIRE. First known county organization 1847; present club 1899. Minor counties champions 1970 and 1972. Beat 2nd XI of a first-class county (Yorkshire) in 1972 in the Championship Challenge match. Its first captain after World War I, Henry Grierson, founded the XL Club.

HERTFORDSHIRE. First known county organization 1838; present club 1876. One of the 7 founders (in 1895) of the Championship, which it won in 1936 and 1975. Became the first minor county to reach the 3rd round of the Gillette Cup when it beat Essex at Hitchin by 33 runs in 1976.

SHROPSHIRE. First known county organization 1819 or 1829; present club 1956. Although among the oldest of today's minor county clubs, not elected to the Championship until 1957. Won it in 1973 under the captaincy of the present chairman, G. V. Othen.

CHESHIRE. First known county organization 1819; present club 1908. Won the Championship in 1967 under the captaincy of Fred Millett.

CORNWALL. First known county organization 1813; present club 1894. One of only 4 counties still to win the Championship, but came close in 1974 when it finished second to Oxfordshire.

LINCOLNSHIRE. First known county organization 1853; present club 1906. Won the Championship in 1966. Became only the second minor county side to defeat a first-class county when it beat Glamorgan by 6 wickets in 1974.

BUCKINGHAMSHIRE. First known county organization 1864; present club 1891. First president was Baron Rothschild. Entered the Minor Counties Championship in 1896 and came second. Shared title in 1899 and has since won outright 7 times. Greatest player between the wars was W. B. Franklin.

WILTSHIRE. First known county organization 1881; present club 1893. Won the Championship in 1902 and 1909. Its best-known players were A. M. Miller and Jesse Smith, who played in the early years of the century.

SUFFOLK. First known county organization 1864; present club 1932. First won the Championship in 1946 and then again in 1977 and 1979. Produced 2 bowlers in the 1960s who went on to play for England: David Larter and Robin Hobbs.

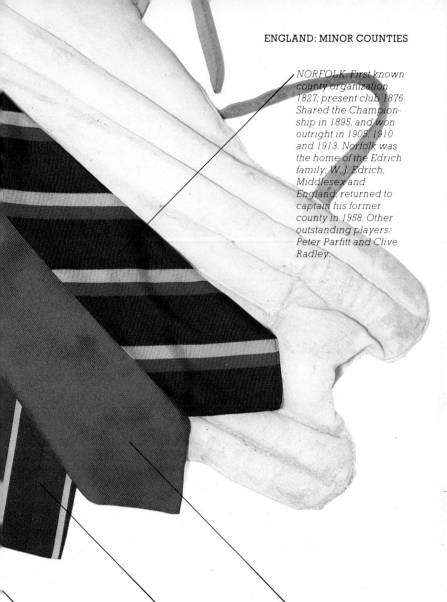

NORFOLK. First known county organization 1827; present club 1876. Shared the Championship in 1895, and won outright in 1905, 1910 and 1913. Norfolk was the home of the Edrich family; W. J. Edrich, Middlesex and England, returned to captain his former county in 1958. Other outstanding players: Peter Parfitt and Clive Radley.

STAFFORDSHIRE. First known county organization 1871; present club 1932. First won the Championship in 1906, and subsequently took the title another 5 times; has not won since 1927. S. F. Barnes ranks among the very greatest bowlers at Test level with 189 wickets in just 27 matches for England before World War I.

OXFORDSHIRE. First known county organization 1787; present club 1921. Won the Championship in 1929 and 1974. One of the founders of the Minor Counties Association, with many fine grounds, notably those of the Oxford colleges. Recent fine players have been M. D. Norton and David Banton.

DURHAM. First known county organization 1874; present club 1882. Shared the title in the first year of the Championship (1895) and again in 1900. Has taken the title 6 times since then (3 times since 1976). Became the first minor county side to defeat a first-class county in the Gillette Cup when it beat Yorkshire in 1973. Among many fine players to go on to a first-class career are Dick Spooner, Colin Milburn and Peter Willey.

33

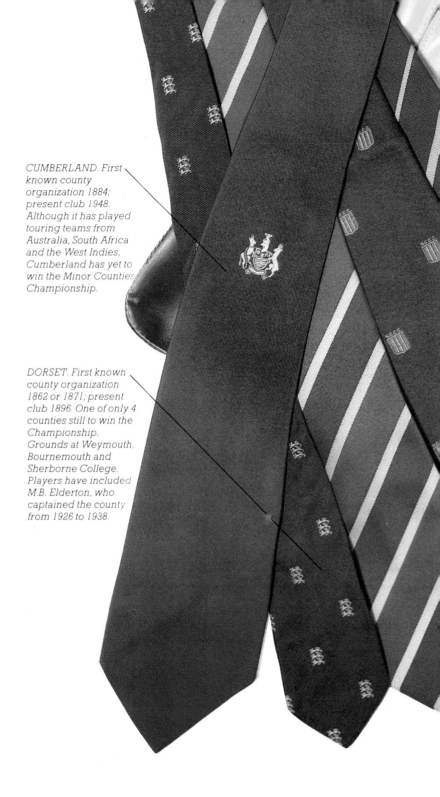

CUMBERLAND. First known county organization 1884; present club 1948. Although it has played touring teams from Australia, South Africa and the West Indies, Cumberland has yet to win the Minor Counties Championship.

DORSET. First known county organization 1862 or 1871; present club 1896. One of only 4 counties still to win the Championship. Grounds at Weymouth, Bournemouth and Sherborne College. Players have included M.B. Elderton, who captained the county from 1926 to 1938.

CAMBRIDGESHIRE. First known county organization 1844; present club 1891. One of the strongest counties during the 1850s and 1860s; in 1864 it beat Yorkshire (twice) and Nottinghamshire. Forced to disband in 1869, it was not formed again until 1891, when it gave Surrey and England 2 immortal opening batsmen: Tom Hayward and Jack Hobbs. Won the Championship in 1963. Cyril Coote, Cambridge University coach, was a county batsman.

BERKSHIRE. First known county organization 1841; present club 1895. First won the Championship in 1924 and again in 1928 and 1953. Owed much to H. L. Lewis, player or secretary over 50 years. Outstanding post-war batsmen were Peter May and Ken Barrington.

NORTHUMBERLAND. First known county organization 1834; present club 1895. Scored most points in the 1924 and 1925 Championships, but in both years lost the Challenge Match and thus failed to take the title. Good players include L. E. Liddell and G. Walton.

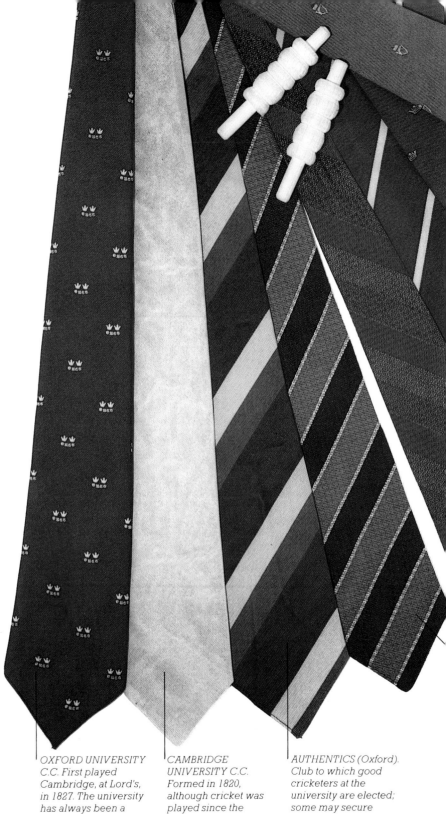

OXFORD UNIVERSITY C.C. First played Cambridge, at Lord's, in 1827. The university has always been a training ground for future England cricketers and captains.

CAMBRIDGE UNIVERSITY C.C. Formed in 1820, although cricket was played since the mid-18th century. Has produced many England players and captains.

AUTHENTICS (Oxford). Club to which good cricketers at the university are elected; some may secure Blues. Its Cambridge counterpart is the Crusaders.

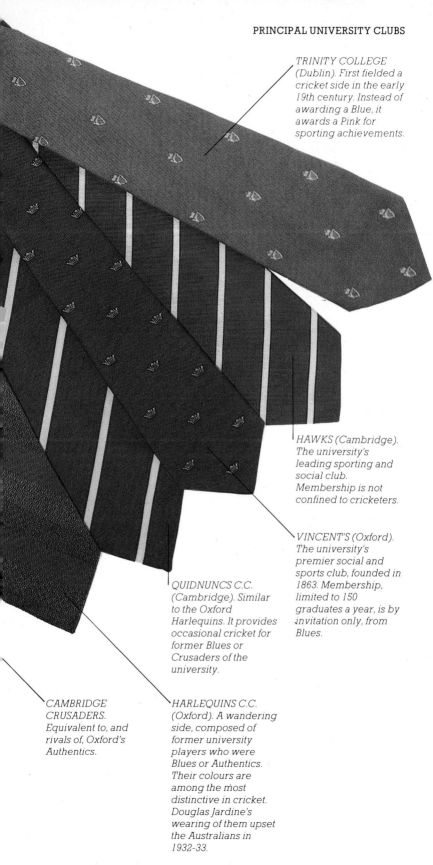

TRINITY COLLEGE (Dublin). First fielded a cricket side in the early 19th century. Instead of awarding a Blue, it awards a Pink for sporting achievements.

HAWKS (Cambridge). The university's leading sporting and social club. Membership is not confined to cricketers.

VINCENT'S (Oxford). The university's premier social and sports club, founded in 1863. Membership, limited to 150 graduates a year, is by invitation only, from Blues.

QUIDNUNCS C.C. (Cambridge). Similar to the Oxford Harlequins. It provides occasional cricket for former Blues or Crusaders of the university.

CAMBRIDGE CRUSADERS. Equivalent to, and rivals of, Oxford's Authentics.

HARLEQUINS C.C. (Oxford). A wandering side, composed of former university players who were Blues or Authentics. Their colours are among the most distinctive in cricket. Douglas Jardine's wearing of them upset the Australians in 1932-33.

HARROW WANDERERS; 1870, from Old Harrovians. Players in the 1st XI automatically become members. Plays a 2-day game against the Eton Ramblers. Its most famous player was F. S. Jackson, one of England's great players in the Golden Age, and later chairman of the England selectors.

ETON RAMBLERS; 1862, from Old Etonians. It has produced many M.C.C. presidents, including Sir William Worsley (1961) and G. O. (Gubby) Allen (1963), the latter a celebrated fast bowler with 25 England caps. This was the first club tie issued (in 1863).

ESTABLISHED CLUBS

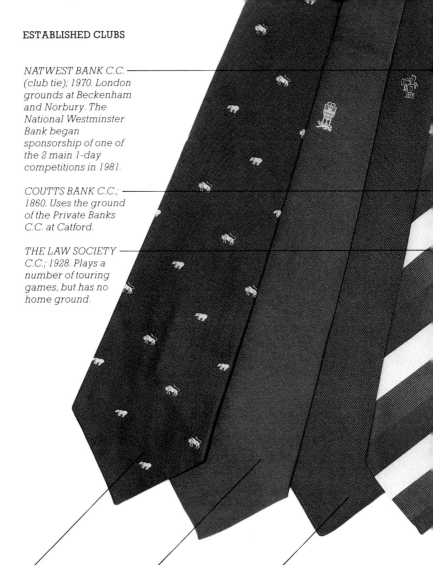

NATWEST BANK C.C. (club tie); 1970. London grounds at Beckenham and Norbury. The National Westminster Bank began sponsorship of one of the 2 main 1-day competitions in 1981.

COUTTS BANK C.C.; 1860. Uses the ground of the Private Banks C.C. at Catford.

THE LAW SOCIETY C.C.; 1928. Plays a number of touring games, but has no home ground.

STOCK EXCHANGE C.C.; 1951. A wandering side, drawn from members of the Exchange, its motifs represent aspects of their business.

THE GREATER LONDON COUNCIL C.C. Team drawn from staff of the G.L.C., with ground at Sutton.

LLOYDS BANK C.C.; 1875. Ground at Beckenham.

MIDLAND BANK C.C.; 1891. London ground at New Beckenham.

PRIVATE BANKS C.C.;
1886. London ground at
Catford.

BANK OF ENGLAND
C.C.; 1907, as a sports
club. One of the
strongest London
clubs, its ground is
used by touring sides
for practice.

BARCLAYS BANK C.C.;
1860. London grounds
at Ealing and Norbury.
One of the strongest
sides in the Club
Cricket Conference.

FENNERS (Cambridge University); 1848. Its home ground, at the university, is one of the most beautiful in England and famous for its batting wicket. In a match against the West Indies in 1950, 1,324 runs were scored in 3 days for the loss of 7 wickets, with David Sheppard and John Dewes, future captain of England, scoring 217 and 183 respectively for Cambridge University.

I ZINGARI; 1845, in London. The oldest of the wandering clubs (the name means 'gypsies' in Italian), its black, red and gold colours symbolize 'Out of darkness, through fire and into light'. Membership is small, as is the annual fixture list.

THE CRICKETERS CLUB OF LONDON; 1964, by Frank Russell, county player and cricket enthusiast. Basically a social club; also plays fixtures.

INCOGNITI C.C.; 1850. Membership is by invitation. This wandering side often tours abroad, particularly to America. Oliver Battock was a distinguished bowler (2,000 wickets) between 1927 and 1970.

FREE FORESTERS C.C.; 1856, in Sutton Coldfield, Warwickshire. With a considerable fixture list, this wandering side is of a very high standard and plays occasional matches having first-class status.

CROSS ARROWS; 1880. It was formed at Lord's for officials and ground staff, and players who learnt their game at the ground. Plays its home fixtures on the Nursery ground at Lord's, in September.

THE CRICKET SOCIETY; 1945, in London, originally the Society of Cricket Statisticians. Worldwide membership, with affiliated clubs in Australia and Zimbabwe. Often tours abroad, either as supporters to the English team, or as a side in its own right. It has a fine library in its London headquarters.

THE ROYAL HOUSEHOLD (City tie); first worn in 1984. Purple, red and gold make up the Queen's colours.

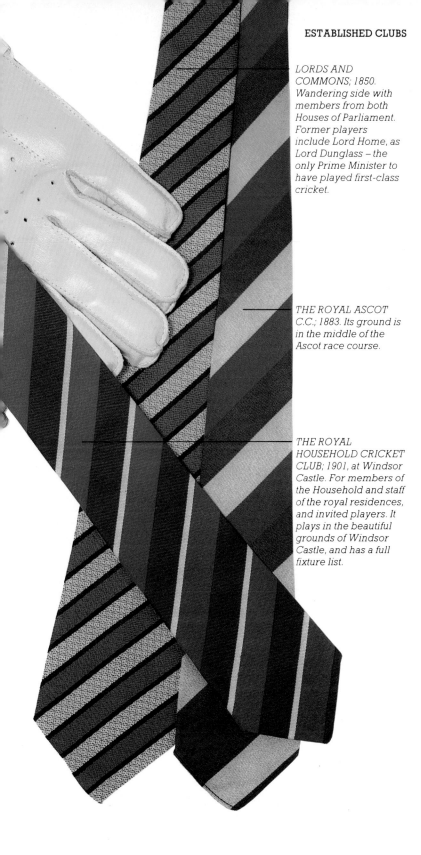

LORDS AND COMMONS; 1850. Wandering side with members from both Houses of Parliament. Former players include Lord Home, as Lord Dunglass – the only Prime Minister to have played first-class cricket.

THE ROYAL ASCOT C.C.; 1883. Its ground is in the middle of the Ascot race course.

THE ROYAL HOUSEHOLD CRICKET CLUB; 1901, at Windsor Castle. For members of the Household and staff of the royal residences, and invited players. It plays in the beautiful grounds of Windsor Castle, and has a full fixture list.

THE HURLINGHAM
C.C. Formed in 1869, it
plays a fine list of
fixtures each year. One
of London's leading
sports clubs, the
Hurlingham Club is
mainly known for
croquet and the tennis
exhibitions it holds
before Wimbledon.

BROADHALFPENNY
BRIGANDS. A Royal
Navy team that plays at
Broadhalfpenny Down,
Hambledon in Hamp-
shire, traditionally the
place where cricket
was first played in the
mid-18th century.

Above: The 'Bat and Ball' public house at Hambledon, Hampshire. According to tradition, the first proper game of cricket was played opposite here in the mid-18th century. A monument, unveiled in 1908, commemorates the event.

SOMERSET WYVERNS. Formed by supporters of the county team who live outside the county, mainly in London, and raise funds to support their side.

THE XL CLUB.
Founded in 1936 by
Henry Grierson.
Membership was
restricted to players
over 40, but now
includes some
younger invited
players. A wandering
side, its patron is the
Duke of Edinburgh.

FRIENDS OF
ARUNDEL CASTLE
C.C. Formed by the
16th Duke of Norfolk as
the Duke of Norfolk's
XI, its name was
changed after his
death in 1975. This tie is
identical to the one
designed for the
original club.

SIR JULIEN CAHN'S XI.
Founded in 1926 by the
millionaire
philanthropist, who
'collected' famous
cricketers. They
played in England and
also visited countries
including Argentina,
Canada and New
Zealand.

Far left: Arundel ground. Lavinia, Duchess of Norfolk has carried on her husband's tradition of staging the first fixture of a visiting side, as well as charity matches, here.

CAPTAIN
R. H. HAWKINS XI.
Formed by the owner of Everdon Hall, Northamptonshire. Many clubs have played there including the Hong Kong XI in 1982.

BAND OF BROTHERS.
Formed in 1858 for men born in, or permanently resident in, Kent. It plays the principal Kent clubs, schools and top-grade wandering sides.

JACK FROST XI.
Formed to play cricket in the winter (hence its name); now also plays in summer. A wandering side, its overseas tours include one to California (the tie for which is shown).

E. W. SWANTON'S XI.
Formed by one of Britain's best-known cricket writers. He took sides to the West Indies in 1956 and 1961. A victorious team which toured the Far East in 1964 included Gary Sobers.

DERRICK ROBINS' XI.
Formed by the Midlands cricket benefactor. Between 1959 and 1979 he took virtually an all-England XI to play in South Africa, South America, Canada, the Near East and Australia.

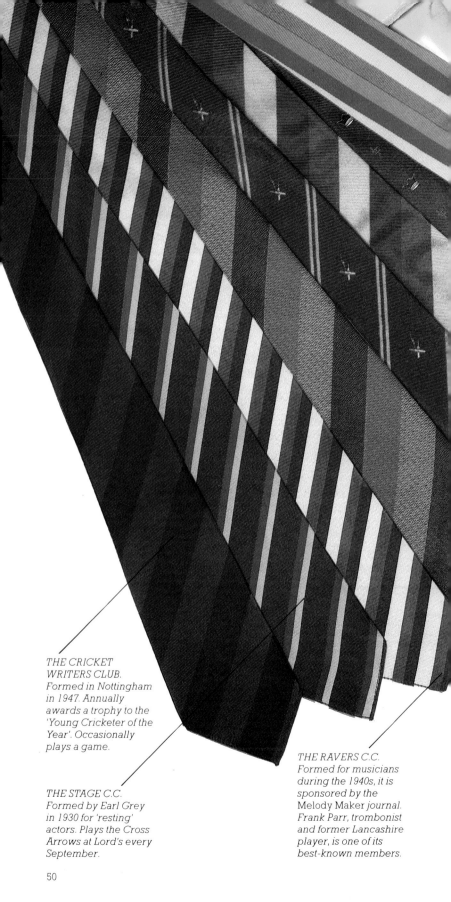

THE CRICKET
WRITERS CLUB.
Formed in Nottingham
in 1947. Annually
awards a trophy to the
'Young Cricketer of the
Year'. Occasionally
plays a game.

THE STAGE C.C.
Formed by Earl Grey
in 1930 for 'resting'
actors. Plays the Cross
Arrows at Lord's every
September.

THE RAVERS C.C.
Formed for musicians
during the 1940s, it is
sponsored by the
Melody Maker journal.
Frank Parr, trombonist
and former Lancashire
player, is one of its
best-known members.

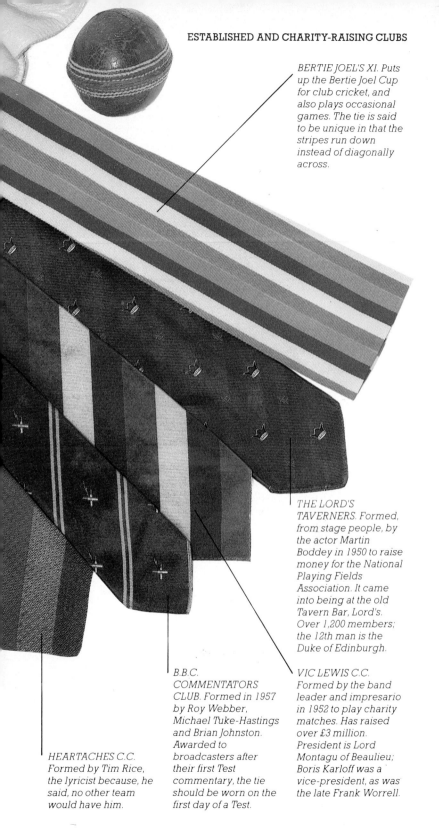

BERTIE JOEL'S XI. Puts up the Bertie Joel Cup for club cricket, and also plays occasional games. The tie is said to be unique in that the stripes run down instead of diagonally across.

THE LORD'S TAVERNERS. Formed, from stage people, by the actor Martin Boddey in 1950 to raise money for the National Playing Fields Association. It came into being at the old Tavern Bar, Lord's. Over 1,200 members; the 12th man is the Duke of Edinburgh.

B.B.C. COMMENTATORS CLUB. Formed in 1957 by Roy Webber, Michael Tuke-Hastings and Brian Johnston. Awarded to broadcasters after their first Test commentary, the tie should be worn on the first day of a Test.

VIC LEWIS C.C. Formed by the band leader and impresario in 1952 to play charity matches. Has raised over £3 million. President is Lord Montagu of Beaulieu; Boris Karloff was a vice-president, as was the late Frank Worrell.

HEARTACHES C.C. Formed by Tim Rice, the lyricist because, he said, no other team would have him.

51

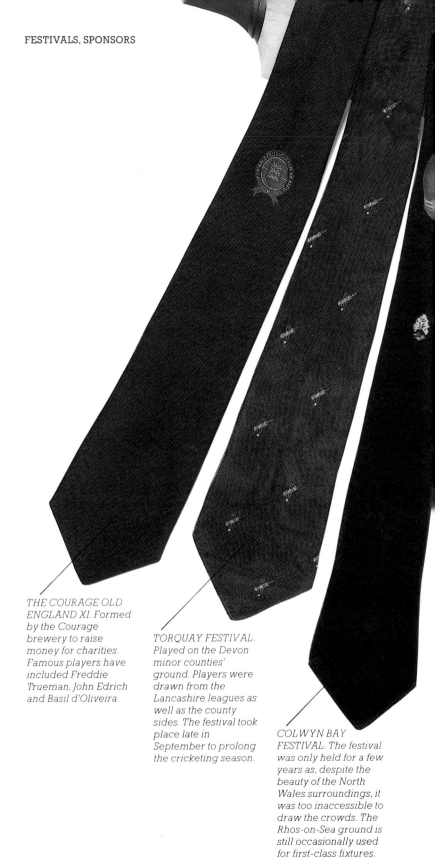

THE COURAGE OLD ENGLAND XI. Formed by the Courage brewery to raise money for charities. Famous players have included Freddie Trueman, John Edrich and Basil d'Oliveira.

TORQUAY FESTIVAL. Played on the Devon minor counties' ground. Players were drawn from the Lancashire leagues as well as the county sides. The festival took place late in September to prolong the cricketing season.

COLWYN BAY FESTIVAL. The festival was only held for a few years as, despite the beauty of the North Wales surroundings, it was too inaccessible to draw the crowds. The Rhos-on-Sea ground is still occasionally used for first-class fixtures.

HASTINGS FESTIVAL.
First held in 1887, it
saw many fine touring
sides, but ended in the
early 1960s because of
poor attendances.

SCARBOROUGH
FESTIVAL. First held
in 1876, it is the only
festival to survive.
Yorkshire plays a
first-class fixture, and
overseas teams usually
end their tour by
playing an England
team here.

THE GILLETTE CUP.
Started in 1963, the first
of the 1-day compe-
titions. Each side was
limited to 60 overs. The
first winner was Sussex
and the last (1980) was
Middlesex. The man of
the match received a
cheque and a tie:
shown is the tie won by
Viv Richards in the
1979 final.

NATWEST BANK TROPHY. Started 1981, as the successor to the Gillette Cup for limited-overs cricket. First winners were Derbyshire. Highest individual score is 111 by Geoff Cook of Northamptonshire (1981 final).

THE JOHN PLAYER LEAGUE. Started 1969, by the tobacco company. The 40-overs-per-side matches have made Sunday cricket highly popular. First winners were Lancashire. 1983 champions: Yorkshire.

THE SCHWEPPES CHAMPIONSHIP. In 1977 the Schweppes Mineral Water Co. became the first sponsor of the County Championship. By 1978 it was known as the Schweppes Championship. Schweppes ended their sponsorship in 1983, and in 1984 Britannic Assurance took over their role.

CORNHILL INSURANCE TEST SERIES. The company's sponsorship of Test cricket in England started in 1978 and has continued ever since.

THE NATIONAL VILLAGE CHAMPIONSHIP. Sponsored by John Haig and Co. from 1972 to 1979, now by Whitbreads. The final is played at Lord's.

THE ENGLISH IN SOUTH AFRICA (Unofficial). In spite of the ban on official visits, an unofficial England side, captained by Graham Gooch, toured South Africa and played international matches there in 1982.

THE PRUDENTIAL
TROPHY. *Started in
1972, it was the first
international limited-
overs tournament.
England plays a series
of 3 matches, each 55
overs per side, against
the touring side.
Prudential support
ended in 1982, and
Texaco sponsored the
1984 series between
England and the West
Indies.*

THE WEST INDIANS IN
SOUTH AFRICA
*(Unofficial). In spite of
the official ban a West
Indian XI, captained by
Lawrence Rowe,
toured South Africa in
1983.*

ASSOCIATION OF SCORERS AND STATISTICIANS. Formed by an often underrated group, it brought a new dimension to the game and its records. Famous names include Roy Webber and Bill Frindall.

THE PRUDENTIAL WORLD CUP, 1983. Started in 1975, these keenly contested 1-day international matches are played every 4 years in England. The West Indies won the cup in 1975 and 1979, but were beaten by outsiders India in a famous upset at Lord's in 1983.

THE WHITBREAD TIE. Since 1979, Whitbread and Co. has continued the sponsorship of the National Village Championship. The Whitbread XI plays a number of games each year for cricketers' benefits.

THE I.C.C. TROPHY, 1979. The competition was first organized in 1979 by associate members of the I.C.C. The 2 winning sides – Canada and Sri Lanka – went forward to the Prudential World Cup.

THE I.C.C. TROPHY, 1982. In 1982 Sri Lanka became a full I.C.C. member and therefore competed in the 1983 Prudential World Cup in its own right. Consequently, only the outright winner of the 1982 I.C.C. Trophy, Zimbabwe, went on to the World Cup.

THE ASSOCIATION OF CRICKET UMPIRES. Formed in 1953 to standardize and maintain the quality of umpiring throughout the world. An extremely high stan-dard of examination performance and practical fieldwork is expected of candidates.

THE PRUDENTIAL WORLD CUP, 1979. The West Indies won the first 2 of these celebrated international 1-day contests, beating Australia in 1975 and England in 1979.

R.K.'s INTERNATIONAL XI. Toured Pakistan in 1981 with a full 'Test' side, playing 3 5-day matches and 3 1-day games. Rohan Kanhai was captain, Michael Holding vice-captain and Vic Lewis manager.

THE ROYAL NAVY C.C. Formed at Plymouth in 1863. The Fleet has been playing cricket since the early 17th century, wherever it went ashore. Each summer the club plays an inter-services tournament against the Army and Royal Air Force.

THE ARMY C.C. Has been playing for over 200 years. First official first-class match against the Royal Navy was at Lord's in 1908. First played the Royal Air Force in 1919.

COMBINED SERVICES C.C. The Army and Royal Navy first played the combined Oxford and Cambridge universities in 1910 and won. Since then the combined services (the Royal Air Force joined in 1920) have played 13 of the 17 counties and most cricket-playing nations.

ROTHMANS CAVALIERS INTERNATIONAL XI. Formed early 1960s. Rothmans, the first sponsor from the tobacco industry, helped to popularize 1-day cricket.

THE ROYAL AIR FORCE C.C. Formed in 1919. First played the Army that year and the Royal Navy in 1920, the beginning of the inter-services tournament. One of its finest players was A. C. Shireff.

ARABS C.C.; 1935, by E. W. Swanton. Many members are Oxford Blues. It has played the Rhine Army and BAFO in Germany, and in the West Indies. First side to fly on tour.

NEW SOUTH WALES CRICKETERS CLUB; early 1960s, in Sydney. After visiting the Cricketers Club in London, Frank Russell, the county player and cricket devotee, decided to form a similar club in Australia, together with members of the Australian side. Mainly a social club.

STRAGGLERS OF ASIA; 1925, at Chail in India. The team was formed by the Northampton-shire Regiment, for servicemen and civilians. The original qualification for membership was one year's residence east of Suez. This wandering side, based in England, regularly plays 1-day matches against forces' sides and the top club teams.

THE AUSTRALIAN CRICKET SOCIETY. Affiliated to The Cricket Society in London, its 7 branches organize dinners, speakers and events to publicize cricket.

Above: Newlands ground in Cape Town. Dominated by the impressive bulk of Table Mountain, it has been played on since 1888. The photograph shows the South Africans playing a West Indian team in 1983.

TRANSVAAL C.C.; 1880s. One of the strongest teams in the interprovincial Currie Cup competition, it originally played in Pretoria. Its ground is now the prestigious Wanderers Club in Johannesburg. Many players, like Bruce Mitchell and Ali Bacher, played for South Africa.

EASTERN PROVINCE
(PORT ELIZABETH
C.C.); 1843. The oldest
club in South Africa, its
best-known players
include the Pollock
brothers, Graeme and
Peter.

SOUTH AFRICA.
One of the founders of
the Imperial Cricket
Conference (1909). It
left the Conference in
1961, but continued
officially to play
international cricket
until 1970, when its tour
to England was
cancelled.

WESTERN PROVINCE
C.C.; late 1880s. Plays at
Newlands, Cape Town,
with Table Mountain
providing a spec-
tacular background.
Famous players have
included Jack
Cheetham and Eddie
Barlow.

SOUTH AFRICAN
CRICKET UNION; 1977.
A multi-racial body, it
officially united
cricketers of all races.
It is not recognized by
the I.C.C.

NATAL C.C.; mid-19th century. One of the strongest sides in South Africa's interprovincial Currie Cup competition. It has produced a long line of famous players, from A. W. Nourse to Barry Richards. Kingsmead, Durban, is its home ground.

UGANDA KOBS; 1920. Uganda's leading club for all sports. Its beautiful ground at Entebbe overlooks Lake Victoria.

KENYA KONGONIS; 1927. The leading organization behind cricket in Nairobi and the rest of the country before the Kenya Cricket Association was formed in 1979.

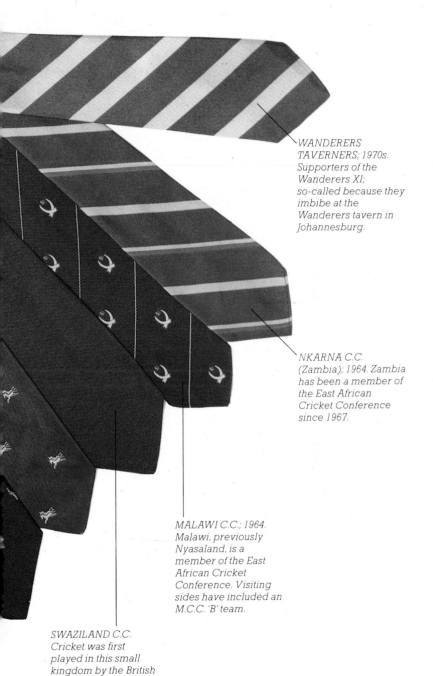

WANDERERS TAVERNERS; 1970s. Supporters of the Wanderers XI; so-called because they imbibe at the Wanderers tavern in Johannesburg.

NKARNA C.C. (Zambia); 1964. Zambia has been a member of the East African Cricket Conference since 1967.

MALAWI C.C.; 1964. Malawi, previously Nyasaland, is a member of the East African Cricket Conference. Visiting sides have included an M.C.C. 'B' team.

SWAZILAND C.C. Cricket was first played in this small kingdom by the British in the 19th century. The motif on the tie is evocative of early African art.

QUEENSLAND C.A.; 1876, in Brisbane. It was the first to join the Board of Control in 1905. Admitted to the interstate Sheffield Shield competition in 1926. Famous players include Ken Mackay, Peter Burge and Ray Lindwall, one of the country's greatest fast bowlers.

AUSTRALIAN CENTENARY TIE. Issued in Melbourne in 1977, to commemorate 100 years of Test cricket between England and Australia.

MELBOURNE C.C.; 1838. The ruling body of Australian cricket until the Board of Control was established in 1905. The present Melbourne ground is the largest in the world, holding 122,000 spectators. Famous players include Bill Ponsford in the 1920s and 1930s, Jack Ryder and Ian Johnson, captain of Australia 1954-57.

NEW SOUTH WALES C.A.; 1826, in Sydney. One of the founders of the Sheffield Shield, in 1882. Players have included Sir Donald Bradman, who scored 340 not out in 1929 as a 20-year-old and 452 not out in 1930, and W. J. O'Reilly.

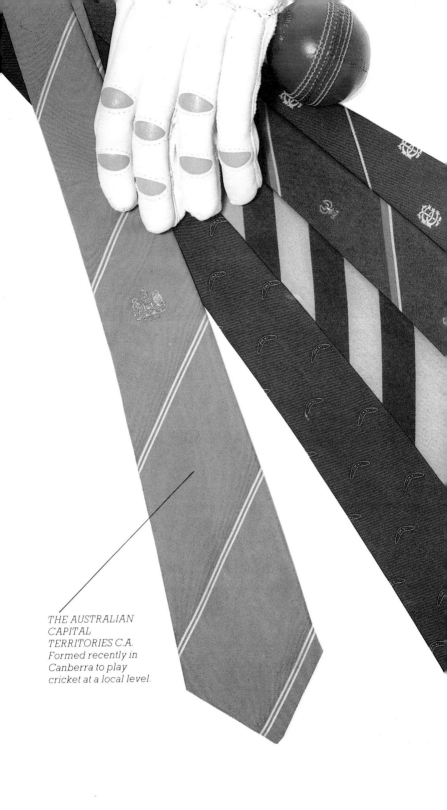

THE AUSTRALIAN
CAPITAL
TERRITORIES C.A.
Formed recently in
Canberra to play
cricket at a local level.

TASMANIA C.A.; early 19th century. A Melbourne side visited the island in the 1850s, but Tasmania was not admitted to the Sheffield Shield until 1977.

SOUTH AUSTRALIA C.A.; 1871, in Adelaide. One of the founders of the Sheffield Shield in 1892, which it won the following year. Famous players include George Giffen, 'the W. G. Grace of Australia' at the end of the last century, and the Chappell brothers, Ian and Gregg, in the 1960s and 1970s.

WESTERN AUSTRALIA C.A.; 1885, in Perth. Admitted to the interstate Sheffield Shield in 1947, it won it 5 times between 1970 and 1978. Many famous players include Dennis Lillee, one of the great Test match fast bowlers, and Kim Hughes, the present Australian captain.

PRIME MINISTER'S XI. Formed by Sir Robert Menzies, a keen cricket supporter. It always played visiting sides. Although this tradition lapsed when Sir Robert died in 1978, it was revived in 1983.

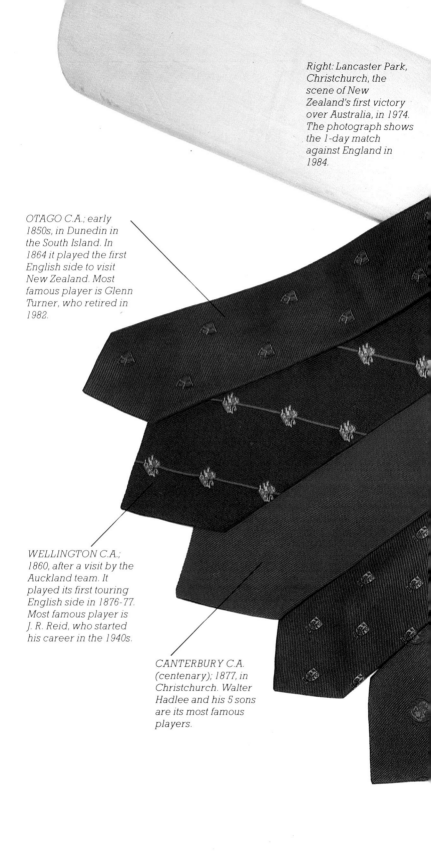

Right: Lancaster Park, Christchurch, the scene of New Zealand's first victory over Australia, in 1974. The photograph shows the 1-day match against England in 1984.

OTAGO C.A.; early 1850s, in Dunedin in the South Island. In 1864 it played the first English side to visit New Zealand. Most famous player is Glenn Turner, who retired in 1982.

WELLINGTON C.A.; 1860, after a visit by the Auckland team. It played its first touring English side in 1876-77. Most famous player is J. R. Reid, who started his career in the 1940s.

CANTERBURY C.A. (centenary); 1877, in Christchurch. Walter Hadlee and his 5 sons are its most famous players.

NEW ZEALAND
CRICKET COUNCIL;
1894, in Christchurch,
by the 4 major
provinces then playing
(Auckland, Canterbury,
Otago and Wellington).
Central Districts
province was admitted
in 1950, and Northern
District in 1956.

AUCKLAND C.A.;
1870s, after a successful
tour of the South Island.
Hedley Howarth is the
first Auckland bowler
to take 300 wickets.
Geoff Howarth, his
brother, is the present
captain.

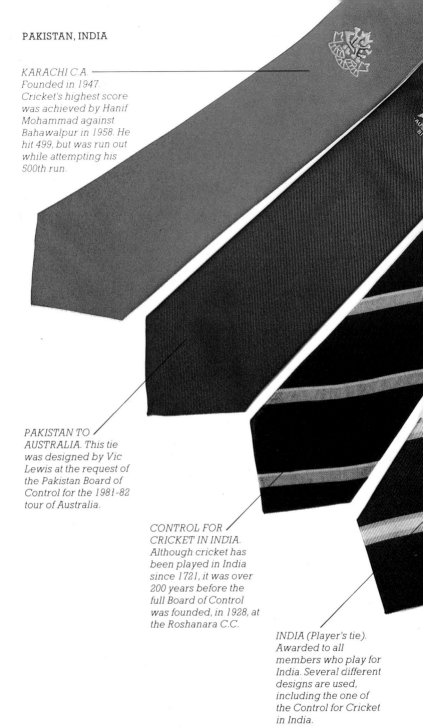

KARACHI C.A.
Founded in 1947.
Cricket's highest score
was achieved by Hanif
Mohammad against
Bahawalpur in 1958. He
hit 499, but was run out
while attempting his
500th run.

PAKISTAN TO
AUSTRALIA. This tie
was designed by Vic
Lewis at the request of
the Pakistan Board of
Control for the 1981-82
tour of Australia.

CONTROL FOR
CRICKET IN INDIA.
Although cricket has
been played in India
since 1721, it was over
200 years before the
full Board of Control
was founded, in 1928, at
the Roshanara C.C.

INDIA (Player's tie).
Awarded to all
members who play for
India. Several different
designs are used,
including the one of
the Control for Cricket
in India.

PUNJAB C.A. Based at Lahore, it is the headquarters of cricket in Pakistan.

DELHI C.A. New Delhi is one of the centres of Test cricket. Its side plays in the Ranji Trophy, which it won for the first time in 1978-79.

NEPAL C.C. Tie presented to Michael Marshall M.P. in the late 1950s, for playing in a side composed of Nepalese army officers and British residents of Nepal against the President of Bengal Cricket Association XI.

Right: Roshanara C.C. ground in Old Delhi. It has provided a background for films as well as cricket matches.

INDIAN PARLIAMENT C.C. Formed by members of both Houses of Parliament, who combine to play an occasional game in Delhi.

ROSHANARA C.C. The founding club of the Control for Cricket in India. Its ground in Old Delhi is one of the most beautiful in the world.

BANDAR MAHSHAHR (Iran). Formed by employees of oil companies. Has ceased to exist following the revolution in Iran.

FIVE Cs. The 'Catch as Catch Can Cricket Club' was formed during World War II in the Suez Canal zone. Membership was mainly British servicemen, but also included invited players. The stripes represent the fines imposed for dropping catches, etc., paid in gold, silver or copper.

DUBAI C.A. In the last 4 or 5 years, it has played exhibition matches with Indian, Pakistani and English sides on an Astro-turf arena. Most members of teams in the Association come from Asia.

BRUNEI C.C. (Borneo). Cricket is played at the Royal Yacht Club, whose tie this is. The club plays mainly against teams from neighbouring Sabah and Sarawak.

KUWAIT C.C. Formed by expatriate employees of the Kuwait Oil Company. It has received visits from many international sides, including Pakistan, England, India and New Zealand.

THE ROYAL BANGKOK SPORTS CLUB (Thailand). Cricket has been played in Thailand since the last century. The club has hosted tours by E. W. Swanton's XI (1964), Worcestershire (1965), and drew a match with an International XI in 1968.

SELANGOR C.C. (Malaysia). Its home base is Kuala Lumpur, a stop-off point for teams travelling between England and Australasia. The club has played most visiting sides.

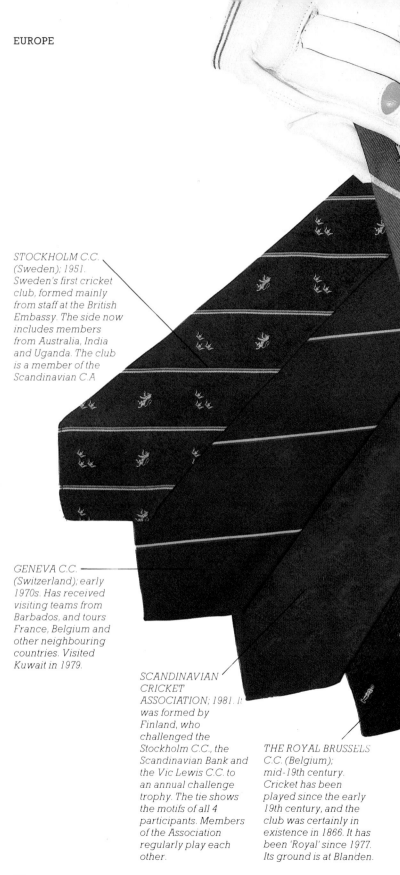

STOCKHOLM C.C.
(Sweden); 1951.
Sweden's first cricket
club, formed mainly
from staff at the British
Embassy. The side now
includes members
from Australia, India
and Uganda. The club
is a member of the
Scandinavian C.A

GENEVA C.C.
(Switzerland); early
1970s. Has received
visiting teams from
Barbados, and tours
France, Belgium and
other neighbouring
countries. Visited
Kuwait in 1979.

SCANDINAVIAN
CRICKET
ASSOCIATION; 1981. It
was formed by
Finland, who
challenged the
Stockholm C.C., the
Scandinavian Bank and
the Vic Lewis C.C. to
an annual challenge
trophy. The tie shows
the motifs of all 4
participants. Members
of the Association
regularly play each
other.

THE ROYAL BRUSSELS
C.C. (Belgium);
mid-19th century.
Cricket has been
played since the early
19th century, and the
club was certainly in
existence in 1866. It has
been 'Royal' since 1977.
Its ground is at Blanden.

HELSINKI C.C. (Finland); 1975, mainly by expatriates from Britain, India and Pakistan. Some Finnish players. Host and founding member (1981) of the Scandinavian Cricket Association.

BLOMENDAAL C.C.
(Holland). Formed in
1910, near Haarlem.

DE FLAMINGOS
(Holland). Formed in
1921, it regularly plays
the M.C.C. and the Free
Foresters. An
interchange with
Oxford University has
recently been
arranged.

*STANDARD ATHLETIC CLUB (France).
Leading sports club in
Paris; the cricket team
was formed by
expatriate British, and
it is believed that there
have been no French
players. The side plays
teams from Holland,
Belgium and England.*

*THE ROME SPORTS
ASSOCIATION (Italy).
The Association
presented this tie to the
Bertie Joel XI when it
toured Rome in the
mid-1970s. The Italian
Cricket Association,
consisting of more than
8 teams throughout
Italy, has since been
formed.*

*COLOGNE C.C.
(Germany). Formed in
the early 1950s by
members of the British
Forces Network. It has
played Rhine Army
base teams and visiting
sides from England.*

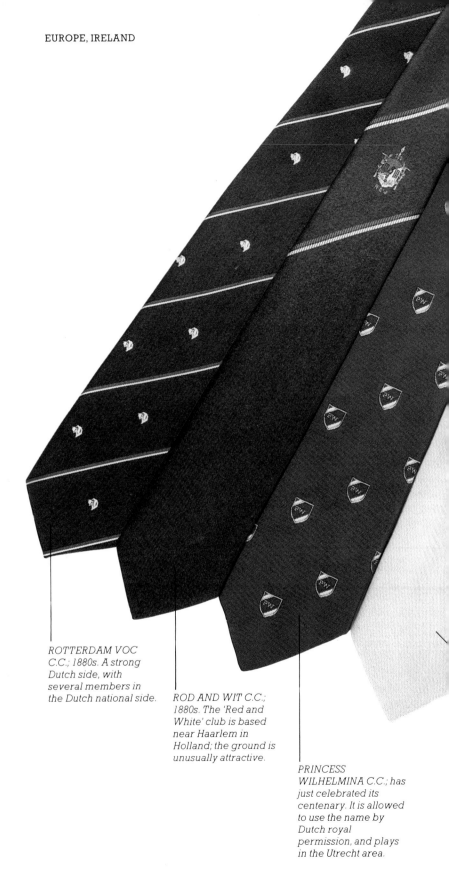

ROTTERDAM VOC C.C.; 1880s. A strong Dutch side, with several members in the Dutch national side.

ROD AND WIT C.C.; 1880s. The 'Red and White' club is based near Haarlem in Holland; the ground is unusually attractive.

PRINCESS WILHELMINA C.C.; has just celebrated its centenary. It is allowed to use the name by Dutch royal permission, and plays in the Utrecht area.

THE MALTA MANIACS;
late 1970s by Bill
Frindall, a B.B.C.
statistician. The basic
colour represents the
sand of Malta; the
motifs are the B.B.C.
lightning flash, the
George Cross of
Malta and crossed bats.
Now tours the
Mediterranean.

THE LEPRECHAUNS
C.C.; 1948. Members
are from Northern
Ireland and the
Republic of Ireland. A
wandering side, it
annually tours
England. Always a
fixture against Essex.

PHOENIX PARK
(Dublin); 1830. The
oldest club in Ireland,
and one of the oldest in
the world. Members of
I Zingari were the first
visitors, in 1851.

QUEBEC C.A. Formed in 1979, when the Quebec Cricket Council joined the Canadian C.A.

CANADIAN OVER FORTIES C.C. The equivalent of the English XL Club, it is open to cricketers when they reach 40.

TORONTO C.C.; 1827. One of Canada's most important clubs, it plays in the Toronto and District C.A. Its match against Merion C.C. (Philadelphia) is an annual fixture. Toured the U.K. in 1982.

ONTARIO C.A.; 1880, as the governing body of cricket in the province.

HURLINGHAM C.C. (Buenos Aires). Cricket has been played in Argentina since the early 19th century, usually by expatriate British, and Hurlingham is one of its most important clubs. The M.C.C. and other British sides have toured many times since 1912.

COLOMBIA C.A. Part of the Bogota Sports Club. Its side is drawn from embassy staff. Hosted a visit by the Derrick Robins XI in 1979.

BRAZIL. Cricket has been played since the 1870s, in Rio de Janeiro, Port Pequeno and São Paulo. Other clubs have since been formed, mainly in Santos and Recife, and Brazil has received visits from M.C.C. 'B' teams. Argentina is its nearest rival.

BRITISH COLUMBIA C.C. Formed in Vancouver, it plays in the Victoria and District League and the British Columbia Mainland League. Frequent tours to the United States.

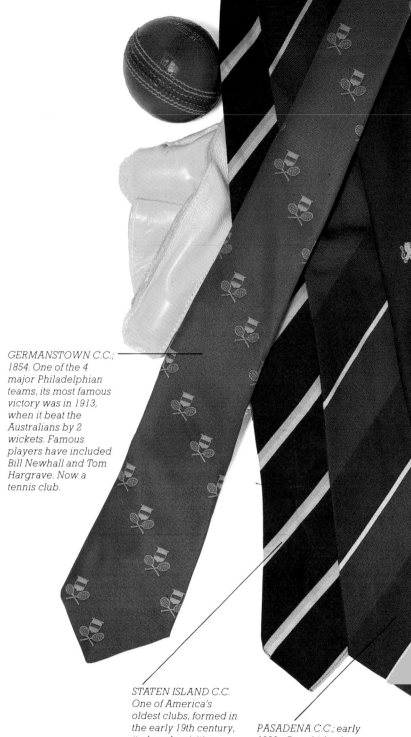

GERMANSTOWN C.C.; 1854. One of the 4 major Philadelphian teams, its most famous victory was in 1913, when it beat the Australians by 2 wickets. Famous players have included Bill Newhall and Tom Hargrave. Now a tennis club.

STATEN ISLAND C.C. One of America's oldest clubs, formed in the early 19th century, it played a visiting English side in 1895. It still plays in the New York League. Many West Indians now play in this League.

PASADENA C.C.; early 1930s. Regularly plays members of the Northern California C.A., and toured Britain in the 1970s. Member of the Southern California C.A.

PHILADELPHIA
PILGRIMS; 1903, in
Scotland, when the
Philadelphia team was
on tour. Members were
Philadelphians who
had played matches
against English or
Australian teams. The
side toured England in
1921.

HOLLYWOOD C.C.;
1932, by Sir C. Aubrey
Smith, who captained
England in South
Africa in 1888. His
enthusiasm made the
side famous, and
encouraged support
for cricket in
California. Players
have included David
Niven and Errol Flynn.
Member of the S.C.C.A.

PRIOR C.C.; 1940s. The
only club still playing
cricket in Philadelphia,
it hosted the M.C.C. 'B'
side for its 2-day
International in 1982.
Its president,
Naseeruddin Khan, is
also president of the
U.S.A.C.A.

STANFORD UNIVERSITY C.C.; 1960. Members include invited players as well as students. The coach is Abid Ali, the Indian Test player. Member of the N.C.C.A., it plays about 25 games a season.

PHILADELPHIA C.C.; 1854. One of the founding clubs of cricket in the United States; now a tennis club. There were 8 Philadelphians in the side that played America's first match against an England XXII at Hoboken, New Jersey, in 1859. America's greatest player, J. Barton King, was a club member; he scored a record 344 against the Merion C.C. 'B' side in 1906.

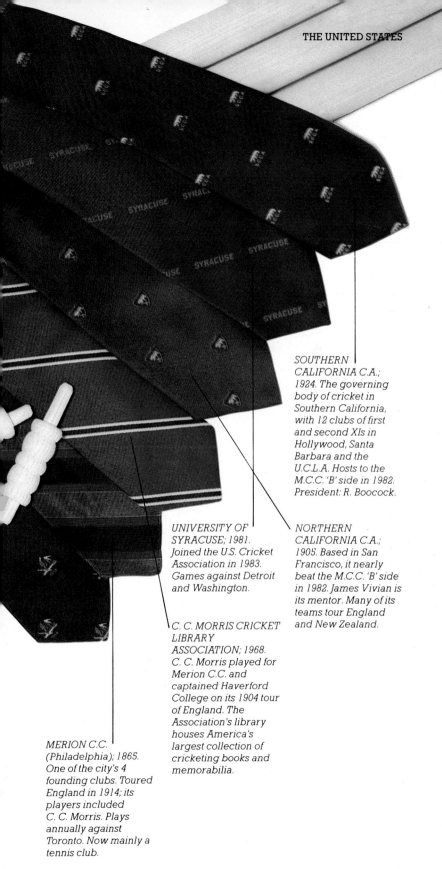

SOUTHERN CALIFORNIA C.A.; 1924. The governing body of cricket in Southern California, with 12 clubs of first and second XIs in Hollywood, Santa Barbara and the U.C.L.A. Hosts to the M.C.C. 'B' side in 1982. President: R. Boocock.

UNIVERSITY OF SYRACUSE; 1981. Joined the U.S. Cricket Association in 1983. Games against Detroit and Washington.

NORTHERN CALIFORNIA C.A.; 1905. Based in San Francisco, it nearly beat the M.C.C. 'B' side in 1982. James Vivian is its mentor. Many of its teams tour England and New Zealand.

C. C. MORRIS CRICKET LIBRARY ASSOCIATION; 1968. C. C. Morris played for Merion C.C. and captained Haverford College on its 1904 tour of England. The Association's library houses America's largest collection of cricketing books and memorabilia.

MERION C.C. (Philadelphia); 1865. One of the city's 4 founding clubs. Toured England in 1914; its players included C. C. Morris. Plays annually against Toronto. Now mainly a tennis club.

SOMERSET C.C. (Bermuda). Crowds of up to 15,000 people flock to the club's annual Cup match with St George's C.C., the sporting and social event of the year in Bermuda.

HONOLULU C.C. (Diamond Head). Cricket was probably introduced by missionaries in the early 19th century. Australia toured in 1932 and Worcestershire in 1965. The diamond head motif is based on a famous landmark.

SAINT GEORGE'S C.C. (Bermuda); late 19th century. It played its first Cup match against Somerset C.C. in 1902. The day of the match has now been designated a public holiday.

HAVERFORD COLLEGE C.C. (Philadelphia); 1834, the first full American-born side. Members of the faculty, male and female, are coached here every summer. The ground will be used for the quarter-finals of the American C.A. in 1984. Its most famous player was C. C. Morris, who captained the side on its tour of England in 1904. It plays in the College Championship.

UNIVERSITY OF
PENNSYLVANIA; 1842,
by W. R. Wister, a
member of the
American team. It won
the College
Championship 17
times between 1881
and 1924. Seven
colleges play in the
competition.

THE UNIVERSITY
CRICKET CLUB OF
LOS ANGELES; 1962. Its
ground is on the
campus on Sunset
Boulevard. The side
has toured England
several times, most
recently in 1983.

Above: The Banks
Brewery Ground
outside Bridgetown,
Barbados. The picture
shows a match
between the Banks
Brewery side and a
team from the south of
the island, in the 1975
Barbados Cricket
League.

BARBADOS C.A.
Cricket has been
played here since the
early 18th century, and
this small island has
produced some of the
game's greatest
names.

KINGSTON C.C. (Jamaica). The club was founded in 1863, and Jamaica played – and won – against an American side in 1887. Famous players include George Headley between the wars and, currently, Michael Holding.

LEEWARD ISLANDS. The islands within the Leeward and Windward Islands had been playing against each other before uniting in 1966. However, they split again and joined the 1980-81 Shell Shield as 2 groups. Their greatest name is Viv Richards of Antigua.

GEORGETOWN C.C. (Guyana). Guyana's first representative side played Barbados in 1865. The Bourda ground has been played on since an American visit in 1886. Many famous players include Rohan Kanhai, Clive Lloyd and Alvin Kallicharran.

QUEENS PARK C.C. (Trinidad). Its ground, the Oval, has been the headquarters of cricket in Trinidad since 1896. Famous players from the island include Learie Constantine and Jeffrey Stollmeyer.

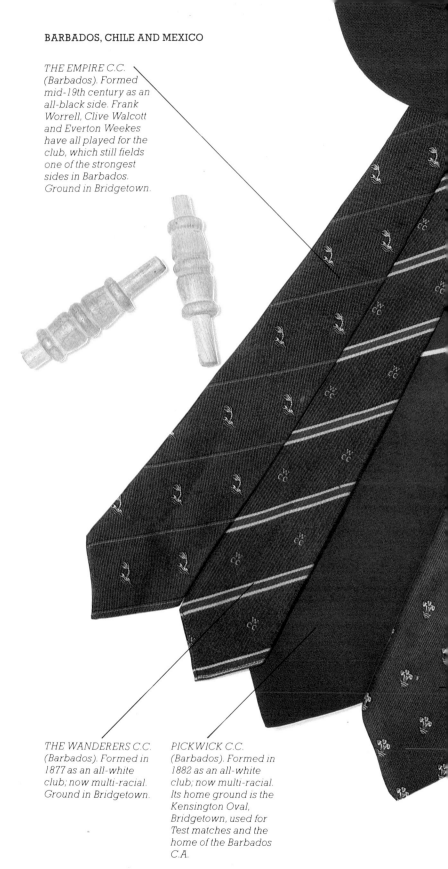

THE EMPIRE C.C. (Barbados). Formed mid-19th century as an all-black side. Frank Worrell, Clive Walcott and Everton Weekes have all played for the club, which still fields one of the strongest sides in Barbados. Ground in Bridgetown.

THE WANDERERS C.C. (Barbados). Formed in 1877 as an all-white club; now multi-racial. Ground in Bridgetown.

PICKWICK C.C. (Barbados). Formed in 1882 as an all-white club; now multi-racial. Its home ground is the Kensington Oval, Bridgetown, used for Test matches and the home of the Barbados C.A.

MEXICO CITY C.C.
Plays visiting teams
from the United States,
Australia and England.

PRINCE OF WALES
COUNTRY CLUB
(Santiago). Cricket has
been played in Chile
since the 1820s,
probably at first by the
Royal Navy, and in
Santiago (against
Valparaiso) since 1870.
The Prince of Wales,
formed by expatriate
British, is the principal
club, and hosted the
Derrick Robins XI in
1979.

SIR GARFIELD SOBERS' 365. The world's finest all-round player was born in Barbados in 1936. The tie commemorates the record individual Test score, 365 not out, made against Pakistan in 1965 when he was 21 years old.

GEOFF BOYCOTT'S 100 HUNDREDS. This controversial figure was born in 1940. He scored his 100th century in 1977 at his home ground of Headingley in Yorkshire, in the 4th Test against Australia.

AMBRIDGE ARCHERS. Formed from the original cast of the B.B.C.'s long-running radio serial, 'The Archers'. It plays several teams in the Birmingham area.

CRICKET CENTENARY TIE v. AUSTRALIA. This commemorates the first home Test match against Australia, in 1880. The motif on the tie, issued by the Test and County Cricket Board, shows the lion and kangaroo with a cricket ball between them.

SIR FRANK WORRELL MEMORIAL TIE. This tie, issued in the West Indies, commemorates one of the most respected cricketers of all time. Born in 1924, he died in 1967.

GLENN TURNER'S 100 HUNDREDS. One of New Zealand's greatest cricketers, born in 1947, he retired early, in 1982. In that year he scored his 100th century by hitting 311 not out for Worcestershire in under 5 hours.

SIR FRANK WORRELL'S (Proposed) TOUR OF SOUTH AFRICA. In 1957 Frank Worrell got as far as selecting an all-black West Indian team, and having a tie designed, before the tour was cancelled for political reasons.

A further selection of ties, with their colours, is given below and on the pages that follow.

BRITISH CRICKET CLUBS

Abbots Langley C.C.
Background: Olive green
Motif: Gold mitres

Aberdeenshire C.C.
Stripes: Dark and light blue divided by narrow yellow

The Adastrians C.C.
Background: Grey
Stripes: Wide black, narrow light blue

Athenians C.C.
Stripes: Purple, green, narrow gold

Blackheath C.C.
Stripes: Chocolate brown, dark green, narrow silver

Blue Mantels
Stripes: Navy blue, Cambridge blue, gold

Boston Ramblers (Brentwood C.C.)
Stripes: Dark red, dark blue, gold

Bromley C.C.
Stripes: Black, narrow pink, sage green

Brondesbury C.C.
Background: Brown
Stripes: White, magenta, gold

Brunswick C.C. (Edinburgh)
Background: Black
Motif: Gold feather and 'BCC'

Buccaneers C.C.
Background: Green
Motif: Crossed scimitars

The Butterflies C.C.
Stripes: Cerise, purple, black

Cheam C.C.
Background: Maroon
Motif: Gold hawks

Chingford C.C.
Background: Green
Stripes: Powder blue, narrow yellow

Cryptics C.C.
Background: Dark blue
Stripes: Narrow purple, green, light blue

The Devon Dumplings C.C.
Stripes: Three wide green, narrow black

Earlybirds C.C.
Background: Green
Motif: Gold birds

Emerity C.C.
Stripes: Black, blue, beige

Gemini C.C.
Stripes: Green, blue, maroon

Gentlemen of Devon
Stripes: Wide blue with red and gold

Gentlemen of Essex
Background: Dark blue
Stripes: Narrow red and gold

The Grasshoppers C.C.
Stripes: Tan, green, narrow royal blue

Hampshire Hawks C.C.
Stripes: Wide scarlet and purple, narrow
black

Hampstead C.C.
Stripes: Powder blue, cerise, black

Hayes C.C.
Background: Navy blue
Motif: Gold horse, rampant, narrow gold
stripe

Honor Oak C.C.
Stripes: Purple, black, silver
or
Background: Blue
Motif: Oak leaf

Ilford C.C.
Background: Black
Stripes: Narrow white, green, yellow, maroon

Ipswich and East Suffolk C.C.
Background: Light green
Stripes: Light blue, red

Isle of Man C.C.
Background: Dark blue
Motif: Three red Manx legs, narrow yellow
lines, 'IOM CC'

Lancashire Second XI Players
Background: Royal blue
Stripes: Green, narrow red

Leicestershire Second XI Players
Background: Green
Motif: Red fox

The Licensed Victuallers C.C.
Background: Dark blue
Motif: Gold crowns, light blue stripe

London, New Zealand C.C.
Background: Dark blue
Motif: Red sword through silver fern leaf

The Moat C.C.
Stripes: Black, red, mauve

Nondescripts C.C.
Motif: Pelican
Stripes: Dark blue, chocolate brown, narrow pink

Old Wykehamists C.C.
Stripes: Black, cerise, blue, gold

Privateers C.C.
Background: Dark blue
Stripes: Narrow white, pale blue, pink, yellow
Touring
Stripes: White, pale blue, pink, yellow

The Purchasers C.C.
Background: Green
Stripes: White, narrow Cambridge blue

Quails C.C.
Background: Pale blue
Stripes: Narrow yellow

Repton Pilgrims C.C.
Stripes: Wide dark blue, gold

Romany C.C.
Stripes: Dark blue, maroon, narrow gold

Rottingdean C.C.
Background: Black
Motif: Gold windmill, '1758'

St Thomas' Hospital C.C.
Background: Dark blue
Motif: Head of Edward VI in light blue

Sevenoaks Vine C.C.
Background: Maroon
Motif: Old-fashioned cricketer

Shepperton, Middlesex
Background: Green
Motif: Three red seaxes within a shield

Sherborne School C.C.
Stripes: Dark brown, dark blue, narrow white

Shrewsbury Saracens C.C.
Stripes: Burgundy, black, blue, gold

Streatham C.C.
Stripes: Black, purple, narrow gold

Stoics C.C.
Stripes: Light blue, maroon, scarlet

Surrey Second XI Players
Background: Maroon
Motif: Crown and shield of Duchy of Cornwall

Sussex Martlets C.C.
Background: Dark blue
Stripes: Narrow light blue and pink

Sutton Coldfield C.C.
Background: Green
Stripes: Narrow blue and white

Thames Ditton C.C.
Background: Blue
Stripes: White bordered by narrow red

Tunbridge Wells C.C.
Stripes: Light and dark blue, dark red

Twickenham C.C.
Background: Dark green
Motif: Silver swans and lines

Uxbridge C.C.
Stripes: Dark green, light grey, wide maroon

Wanstead C.C.
Stripes: Black, mauve, narrow yellow and white

West Norfolk C.C.
Background: Green
Stripes: Narrow blue, gold, red

West of Scotland C.C.
Stripes: Blue, maroon, pink

Winchmore Hill C.C.
Stripes: Black, purple, narrow silver

Yellowhammers C.C.
Stripes: Wide black and gold, narrow silver

IRELAND

Clontarf C.C. (Dublin)
Background: Dark blue
Stripes: Red, light blue, black

Cork C.C.
Stripes: Wide light green and light blue, narrow yellow

The Leinster C.C. Centenary Tie
Background: Maroon
Motif: Quartered shield, containing harp

Woodvale C.C. (Belfast)
Stripes: Royal blue, orange, black

CRICKET SOCIETIES

The Council of Cricket Societies
Background: Dark blue
Motif: Three red stumps, ball, 'CCS'

Hampshire Cricket Society
Background: Green or blue
Motif: Three stumps, red rose, 'HCS'

Irish Cricket Society
Stripes: Red, green

Lancashire and Cheshire Cricket Society
Background: Dark blue
Motif: Bushels of hay, red rose

The Northern Cricket Society
Background: Royal blue
Motif: Crossed red and white roses

The Scottish Cricket Society
Background: Blue
Motif: Old Father Time with two Scottish thistles
Players tie
As above but with colours reversed

Sheffield Cricket Lovers Society
Background: Dark blue
Motif: Light blue crest

Wombwell Cricket Society *(Original Tie)*
Background: Blue
Motif: Unicorn

AUSTRALIA

Mossman and District C.C.
Background: Dark blue
Motif: Red whales

North Melbourne C.C.
Background: Dark blue
Motif: Shield with small 'MCC' over large 'M'

W.S.C. (Kerry Packer Australian Internationals)
Stripes: Red, yellow, narrow blue
Players tie
Background: Blue
Motif: Red ball within inverted stumps and bails

DUBAI

Darjeeling C.C.
Background: Green
Motif: Gold eagle and dhow

EUROPE

The Hilversum C.C. (Holland)
Background: Dark blue
Motif: Double-headed eagle, narrow light blue and yellow stripes

The Optimists C.C. (Luxembourg)
Background: Blue
Motif: Stumps, bat and ball, narrow red, white and blue stripes (national colours)

INDIA

Assam C.A.
Background: Green
Motif: 'ACA' in silver stripe

Ballygunge C.C. (Calcutta)
Stripes: Wide dark blue, medium light blue, narrow white

Hyderabad Blues C.C.
Background: Dark blue
Motif: Springing lion, 'HBCC'

Karanataka State C.A. (Bangalore)
Background: Dark blue
Motif: 'KSCA' and bird

Madhya Pradesh C.A. (Indore)
Background: Dark blue
Motif: Red 'MPCA' and stripes

Punjab C.A.
Background: Blue
Motif: 'PCA' and tiger's head

SOUTH AFRICA

The Grasshoppers C.C. (Natal)
Background: Red
Motif: Gold grasshoppers

Griqualand West C.C.
Background: Blue
Motif: Silver diamond

North East Transvaal
Background: Navy blue
Motif: 'NE' divided by protea flower

EAST AFRICA

Tanganyika Twigas
Background: Green
Motif: Brown giraffe at blue water

THE WEST INDIES AND GRAND BAHAMAS

Carlton C.C. (Barbados)
Background: Maroon
Motif: Silver and gold sphinx

Harrison College (Barbados)
Stripes: Wide maroon and dark blue, narrow gold

Luckaya C.C. (Grand Bahamas)
Background: Blue
Motif: Swordfish jumping from water, 'LCC
Grand Bahamas'

Spartan C.C. (Barbados)
Background: Dark blue
Stripes: Gold

PERIODICALS

The Cricketer (magazine)
Background: Navy blue
Motif: Cricketer in white

The Cricketer Country Tie
Background: Green
Motif: Cricketer in fawn

Wisden Monthly (magazine)
Background: Blue
Motif: Old-fashioned players, 'WCM'

LEAGUES AND ASSOCIATIONS

The Central Lancashire League
Background: Green
Stripes: Narrow gold and black, letters 'CLL'

Isle of Wight Cricket Association
Background: Green
Motif: Two narrow gold stripes and gold map
of the Isle of Wight, 'IWCCA'

Lancashire Cricket League
Background: Blue
Motif: Red rose, 'LCC'

Note: Colours of ties may vary, depending on
the material used. If the shade of a tie that you
own doesn't match the one in a photograph,
the reason could well be that it was made
from a different fabric.

Bibliography

The Club Cricket Conference Handbook,
The Club Cricket Conference, Annual.

*The Golden Jubilee Board of Control for
India*, India Board of Control for Cricket, 1979.

J. A. Lester, *A Century of Philadelphia
Cricket*, University of Pennsylvania Press, 1951.

C. Martin-Jenkins, *The Complete Who's Who
of Test Cricketers*, Orbis, 1980.

The Northern and Southern California
Association Annuals.

E. W. Swanton, *Barclays World of Cricket*,
Collins, 1980.

Wisden Cricketers' Almanack, John Wisden,
Annual.

Index

INDEX

ACKNOWLEDGEMENTS

Our thanks to Don Nicholson of Hawkley
Studio Assocs. Ltd. for taking all the
photographs of the ties in this book. We
would also like to thank the following:
All-Sport Photographic Ltd. 62, 71;
The Bridgeman Art Library 6-7 (bottom);
Patrick Eagar 6-7 (top), 13, 22-23, 48;
Vic Lewis 47, 92; Ian Wright 75.